Nearly all rich and powerful people are not notably talented, educated, charming or good-looking.

Φ

For Toni.

They become rich and powerful by wanting to be rich and powerful.

Your vision of where or who you want to be is the greatest asset you have.

Without having a goal it's difficult to score.

CONTENTS.

THE FUNDAMENTALS.

IF YOU CAN'T SOLVE A PROBLEM, IT'S BECAUSE YOU'RE PLAYING BY THE RULES.

GIVE YOURSELF SOME SPIN.

AND NOW FOR A COMMERCIAL BREAK.

YOU DON'T HAVE TO BE CREATIVE TO BE CREATIVE.

NEW BUSINESS.

FINAL THOUGHTS.

WHY DO WE STRIVE FOR EXCELLENCE WHEN MEDIOCRITY IS REQUIRED?

THERE is little demand in the commercial world for excellence. There is a much, much bigger demand for mediocrity.

The truth is, I'm glad it's this way.

Imagine a world where all clients were wonderful, where we could produce whatever we felt like with no restrictions, with everybody having freedom to produce all their fantasies unfettered by tedious clients.

What would we do?

We would react against it, saying, 'Isn't this boring. How can we be dull? Let's do it badly, let's make it ugly, and let's make it really cheaply.'

That's the nature of the creative person. All creative people need something to rebel against, it's what gives their lives excitement, and it's creative people who make the clients' lives exciting.

I do it for me.

SO HOW GOOD DO YOU WANT TO BE?

Quite good.

Good.

Very good.

The best in your field.   The best in the world.

ALL of us want to be good at our jobs, but how good do we really want to be?

Quite good.

Good.

Very good.

The best in our field.

Or the best in the world?

Talent helps, but it won't take you as far as ambition.

Everybody wants to be good, but not many are prepared to make the sacrifices it takes to be great.

To many people, being nice in order to be liked is more important. There's equal merit in that, but you must not confuse being good with being liked.

Most people are looking for a solution, a way to become good.

There is no instant solution, the only way to learn is through experience and mistakes.

You will become whoever you want to be.

It could be you.

Where do you see yourself?

YOU CAN ACHIEVE THE UNACHIEVABLE.

FIRSTLY you need to aim beyond what you are capable of.

You must develop a complete disregard for where your abilities end.

Try to do the things that you're incapable of.

If you think you're unable to work for the best company in its sphere, make that your aim.

If you think you're incapable of running a company, make that your aim.

If you think you're unable to be on the cover of *Time* magazine, make it your business to be there.

Make your vision of where you want to be a reality.

Nothing is impossible.

'I WANT TO BE AS FAMOUS AS PERSIL AUTOMATIC*.'

Victoria Beckham

AS A teenager, Victoria Beckham's ambition was not just to be better than her mates or even be a famous singer but to become a world brand.

She not only dreamed about it, but wanted it enough to go about getting it. That in itself makes her different from most of us.

It's not how good she was that mattered, it's how good she wanted to be.

What is interesting in her quote is that she didn't compare herself with George Michael or Mariah Carey, rather she saw the fame of Persil Automatic as her yardstick.

Laugh at it as you may, it's this highly original imagination that got her where she is today.

* One of the UK's leading detergents.

You know who.

HAVE YOU NOTICED HOW THE CLEVEREST PEOPLE AT SCHOOL ARE NOT THOSE WHO MAKE IT IN LIFE?

WHAT you learn at school are facts, known facts.

Your job at school is to accumulate and remember facts. The more you can remember, the better you do.

SEE THIS BOY?

Those who fail at school are not interested in facts; or maybe the facts are not put to them in a way they find interesting.

Some people simply don't have a great faculty for memory.

It doesn't mean they are stupid. It means their imagination hasn't been fired up by academic tuition.

People who are conventionally clever get jobs on their qualifications (the past), not on their desire to succeed (the future).

Very simply, they get overtaken by those who continually strive to be better than they are.

As long as the goal is there, there is no limit to anyone's achievement.

HE'S ALREADY INTO PUBLICITY.

The Fundamentals.

ENERGY.

IT'S 75% of the job.
If you haven't got it, be nice.

DO NOT SEEK PRAISE. SEEK CRITICISM.

IT IS quite easy to get approval if we ask enough people, or if we ask those who are likely to tell us what we want to hear.

The likelihood is that they will say nice things rather than be too critical. Also, we tend to edit out the bad so that we hear only what we want to hear.

So if you have produced a pleasantly acceptable piece of work, you will have proved to yourself that it's good simply because others have said so.

It is probably ok. But then it's probably not great either.

If, instead of seeking approval, you ask, 'What's wrong with it? How can I make it better?', you are more likely to get a truthful, critical answer.

You may even get an improve-
ment on your idea.

And you are still in a position to
reject the criticism if you think it
is wrong.

Can you find fault with this?

IT'S ALL MY FAULT.

IF YOU are involved in something that goes wrong, never blame others. Blame no one but yourself.

If you have touched something, accept total responsibility for that piece of work.

If you accept responsibility, you are in a position to do something about it.

Here are some common excuses for failure:

1. *It was a terrible brief.*
2. *I need a better partner.*
3. *There wasn't enough money to do it properly.*
4. *The director didn't listen to me.*
5. *I was too busy on other projects.*
6. *I wasn't given enough time.*
7. *The client took out the best ideas.*

Most of these grievances are every day on every job. That won't change.

The point is that, whatever other people's failings might be, you are the one to shoulder the responsibility.

There are no excuses.

The goose blames the boy, the boy blames the goose.

DO NOT COVET YOUR IDEAS.

Give away everything you know, and more will come back to you.

———————

YOU will remember from school other students preventing you from seeing their answers by placing their arm around their exercise book or exam paper.

It is the same at work, people are secretive with ideas. 'Don't tell them that, they'll take the credit for it.'

The problem with hoarding is you end up living off your reserves. Eventually you'll become stale.

If you give away everything you have, you are left with nothing. This forces you to look, to be aware, to replenish.

Somehow the more you give away the more comes back to you.

Ideas are open knowledge. *Don't claim ownership.*

They're not your ideas anyway, they're someone else's. They are out there floating by on the ether.

You just have to put yourself in a frame of mind to pick them up.

The hoarder. She's already reducing her capabilities.

DON'T LOOK FOR THE NEXT OPPORTUNITY. THE ONE YOU HAVE IN HAND IS THE OPPORTUNITY.

WE ARE always waiting for the perfect brief from the perfect client.

It almost never happens.

You're probably working on a job or project right now and saying, 'This is boring, let's just deal with it and get it over with. We'll make the next one good.'

Whatever is on your desk right now, that's the one. Make it the best you possibly can.

It may not be great, but at least you'll have the satisfaction of knowing you did the best you possibly could, and you may learn something from it.

And you're always free to do an alternative that does satisfy your creative standards.

Good briefs don't just come along.

That's true, even if you've earned a reputation for doing good work (although that helps).

Successful solutions are often made by people rebelling against bad briefs.

ACCENTUATE THE POSITIVE.

FIND out what's right about your product or service and then dramatize it, like a cartoonist exaggerates an action.

For example, you know a horse can jump a ditch, therefore you accept that it can jump the Grand Canyon.

This realization accelerated my career faster than anything I have learnt since.

Providing there is a basic truth in your idea, you can dramatize it to infinity.

Here's an example:

A radio commercial for suntan lotion. An Englishman's voice tells of the product's benefits. As he talks his voice gradually changes to that of a West Indian man.

Written by Ron Collins

Brilliant.

You know a suntan lotion won't make you black, but you accept that it might make you brown.

ELIMINATE THE NEGATIVE.

AVOID knocking the competition.

It usually serves to publicize them rather than you.

It may win attention, it may win awards but the likelihood is that it won't win sales.

(It's also much easier to do.)

DO NOT PUT YOUR CLEVERNESS IN FRONT OF THE COMMUNICATION.

CREATIVE people are paid to be creative.

So, in order to justify their salaries, they need to be seen to have clever ideas.

I have no argument with intuitive, clever ideas. These are often the best. The problem is that good ideas do not always come along, great ideas even less often.

In their need to prove their worth, creative people often produce work which on the surface appears clever but has little substance.

Instead of trying to find a quick fix, if they were to spend time finding out what the problem was, they would discover the solution.

In other words, if you ask the

right question, you get the right answer.

There is a book which was written in the 1950s but is still relevant today. It's called *A Technique for Producing Ideas* by James Webb-Young.

It doesn't give you ideas, but it helps sort out what you want to say and helps you arrive at an original and relevant solution.

A clever idea or a logical thought?

DON'T PROMISE WHAT YOU CAN'T DELIVER.

WHEN selling our ideas, we tend to overpromise in our enthusiasm for our creation.

In our vision of how we hope it will be, we leave no room for failure.

The result will probably be disappointing. Not disastrous, but a little less than expected.

No one will say anything, they just won't trust you quite as much next time.

Basically you've blown it.

If instead you undersell, pointing out the possible weaknesses and how to resolve them, should they occur, you are not only building a trusting relationship with your client but you're able to solve any problems.

And if it does turn out the way you hoped, it is a bonus.

Would you use this architect again?

KNOW YOUR CLIENT'S AIMS.

MOST clients are corporate people protecting their own mortgages.

They mistakenly see ideas as a risk rather than an advancement to their careers.

Therefore their motivation may be quite different from their brief to you.

Find out what the client's real objective is.

All clients aspire to status.

It may be their desire to become a member of the New York Yacht

Club or the Jockey Club.

Or to be seen at the best table at Le Cirque or the Ivy.

Or a patron of the arts.

To be chairman of the company.

Owner of a football club.

Or simply a butterfly collector.

These aspirations will never be put into the brief, of course.

For six months we worked on a government scheme devised to help school leavers get jobs.

The best people in the agency worked with passion to help solve a social problem.

The resulting work was marvellous, and there was a lot of it.

It was rejected. All of it.

We had failed to understand, not the brief, but the politics that lay behind it.

All the minister wanted was for the public to know he was spending x millions on advertising for the scheme. To let people know he was doing something about it.

It was a PR exercise for him.

It had nothing at all to do with humanity.

WHAT DO YOU DO WHEN YOUR CLIENT WON'T BUY?

Do it his way. Then do it your way.

A CLIENT often has a fair idea of what he wants.

If you show him what you want and not what he wants, he'll say that's not what he asked for.

If, however, you show him what he wants first, he is then relaxed and is prepared to look at what you want to sell him.

You've allowed him to become magnanimous instead of putting him in a corner.

Give him what he wants and he may well give you what you want.

There is also the possibility that he may be right.

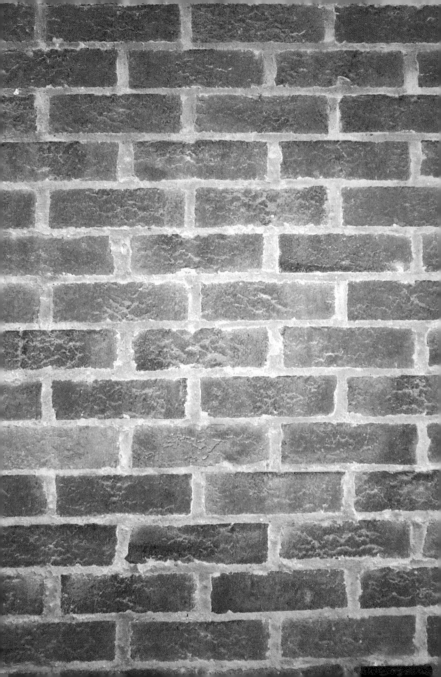

DON'T TAKE NO FOR AN ANSWER.

No Salesmen.

WE HAD been pitching for a sizeable and important government account.

We were in competition with five other companies.

For three months we worked on our campaign.

Then at 5 pm one Wednesday evening we were told we were not on the shortlist of three.

The client gave reasons why.

Normally we say, well tough, on to the next one. Not this time.

I went to our chief executive* and said, 'Call the client to tell him that we have another campaign prepared. Say you'll be in his office with it at 9 am tomorrow morning.'

We didn't have another campaign.

But by 8 am the next morning we had a completely new concept addressing the negatives he had found in the first one.

At 9 am it was presented.

On Friday evening we heard we had won the business.

It was a good weekend.

* The CEO was Paul Bainsfair.

WHEN IT CAN'T BE DONE, DO IT. IF YOU DON'T DO IT, IT DOESN'T EXIST.

A NEW idea can be either unfamiliar, or silly, or both.

It can't be judged by description. It needs to be done (made) to exist.

It is unlikely that anyone will sanction the cost of something they don't understand, therefore you have no choice but to do it yourself.

At whatever cost.

You may have to beg, steal and borrow to get it done. But that's for you to work out how you do it.

It's exciting.

It's difficult and it's fun.

If it was easy anyone could do it.

The film *Citizen Kane* is a very

good example. It was stolen not sanctioned.

Orson Welles could not find any backers, but he did raise a small sum for casting.

He begged, borrowed and cajoled people into building sets and shooting full-blown screen tests which eventually formed a third of the film.

IT EXISTED.

Backers could see what they were getting. He got the money.

Without him doing it when it supposedly couldn't be done, it would be another in the endless list of ideas that never happened.

The Kane Mutiny.

If you can't solve a problem, it's because you're playing by the rules.

THE PEROSN WHO DOESN'T MAKE MISTAKES IS UNLIKELY TO MAKE ANYTHING.

BENJAMIN Franklin said, 'I haven't failed, I've had 10,000 ideas that didn't work.'

Thomas Edison said, 'Of the 200 light bulbs that didn't work, every failure told me something that I was able to incorporate into the next attempt.'

Theatre director Joan Littlewood said, 'If we don't get lost, we'll never find a new route.'

All of them understood that failures and false starts are a precondition of success.

At the last company I worked for

you would not be fired for being wrong, but you would be fired for not having initiative.

It had a positive attitude to mistakes. It was a great company.

Failure was a major contributor to its success.

You may have noticed that the spelling in the headline is incorrect.

This was not an intentional idea.

Lucinda made a typing error.

It was fortuitous that it happened on this page.

'THERE IS NOTHING THAT IS A MORE CERTAIN SIGN OF INSANITY THAN TO DO THE SAME THING OVER AND OVER AND EXPECT THE RESULTS TO BE DIFFERENT.'

Einstein

'FAIL, FAIL AGAIN.

FAIL BETTER.'

Samuel Beckett

IT'S WRONG TO BE RIGHT.

BEING right is based upon knowledge and experience and is often provable.

Knowledge comes from the past, so it's safe. It is also out of date. It's the opposite of originality.

Experience is built from solutions to old situations and problems. The old situations are probably different from the present ones, so that old solutions will have to be bent to fit new problems (and possibly fit badly). Also the likelihood is that, if you've got the experience, you'll probably use it.

This is lazy.

Experience is the opposite of being creative.

If you can prove you're right, you're set in concrete. You cannot move with the times or with other people.

Being right is also being boring. Your mind is closed. You are not open to new ideas. You are rooted in your own rightness, which is arrogant. Arrogance is a valuable tool, but only if used very sparingly.

Worst of all, being right has a tone of morality about it. To be anything else sounds weak or fallible, and people who are right would hate to be thought fallible.

So: it's wrong to be right, because people who are right are rooted in the past, rigid-minded, dull and smug.

There's no talking to them.

IT'S RIGHT TO BE WRONG.

START being wrong and suddenly anything is possible.

You're no longer trying to be infallible.

You're in the unknown. There's no way of knowing what can happen, but there's more chance of it being amazing than if you try to be right.

Of course, being wrong is a risk.

People worry about suggesting stupid ideas because of what others will think.

You will have been in meetings where new thinking has been called for, at your original suggestion.

Instead of saying, 'That's the kind of suggestion that leads us to a novel solution', the room goes quiet, they look up to the ceiling, roll their eyes and return to the discussion.

Risks are a measure of people. People who won't take them are trying to preserve what they have.

People who do take them often end up by having more.

Some risks have a future, and some people call them wrong. But being right may be like walking backwards proving where you've been.

Being wrong isn't in the future, or in the past.

Being wrong isn't anywhere but being here.

Best place to be, eh?

DON'T BE AFRAID OF SILLY IDEAS.

WE ALL get mental blocks.

We need to get unblocked.

The way to get unblocked is to lose our inhibitions and stop worrying about being right.

The comedian John Cleese puts it rather more eloquently, 'High creativity is responding to situations without critical thought' (playfulness).

If you are in deadlock here are a couple of tricks you might try.

1. Do the opposite of what the solution requires.

2. Look out of the window and whatever catches your eye, a bird, a television aerial, an old man on crutches or whatever, make that the solution to your problem.

Maybe the next spread will help you with your illogic.

THIERRY *and* GUY

2001

FAT *bastard*

CHARDONNAY

Aged in Oak barrels

Vin de Pays d'Oc

Alc. 13.5% By Vol.   Produce of France   750 ml
MIS EN BOUTEILLE A F 84190 PAR DDS
NÉGOCIANT-VINIFICATEUR AU CHÂTEAU CANET, RUSTIQUES (AUDE) FRANCE

12797

It is the daft and inelegant name that has made this French wine an
international success in just six years.

Engelbert Humperdinck

A very silly name, but he's nobody's fool.

You won't remember this.

You won't forget this.

Give yourself some spin.

PLAY YOUR CARDS RIGHT.

THE person in the left column is the same person as the one in the right column. But we regard them very differently.

The person in the left column is saying what he is.

The person in the right column is more ambitious. It's how he wants others to perceive him.

How you perceive yourself is how others will see you.

When Charles Saatchi started his ad agency it was regarded as a creative boutique.

His brief for the company stationery was to make it look like a bank. (About fifteen years later they tried to buy a bank.)

He also invested a third of his capital in a full-page advertisement in *The Times*.

The effect was to make his creative boutique appear an established company.

John Ranson

PUMP ATTENDANT

John C. Ranson

PETROLEUM EXECUTIVE

Anthony Taylor

ARCHITECT

Anthony Taylor

ARCHITECTS

Arthur Edburg Jnr.

**DEPUTY VICE PRESIDENT
WITH SPECIAL RESPONSIBILITY
FOR SUB DIVISION 2**

Art Edburg

DIRECTOR

Theodore Smith

CHAIRMAN &
CHIEF EXECUTIVE
(WORLDWIDE)

Theodore Smith. Owner. (no card)

IT'S NOT WHAT YOU KNOW.

YOU all know this old maxim but do you ever think about it.

Consider:

I am a talented architect working for a prestigious company.

Richard Rogers Partnership, for instance.

The company knows my value, respects me and pays me accordingly, but nobody outside the company knows me.

I have buried myself in my work.

You, however, are a first year student at the Architectural Institute.

You print a business card with the

IT'S WHO YOU KNOW.

words: Anthony Taylor. Architect. Or even better Architects.

You are in a bar chatting, you talk yourself up and present your credentials, i.e. your business card.

You will be accepted as an authority or practitioner of architecture.

I, on the other hand, with my lack of social skills and reluctance to push myself forward, will be unnoticed. A nobody.

Unfair as it may seem, this is the reality of life.

If you know what the tricks are, you can play your cards right.

DON'T GIVE A SPEECH. PUT ON A SHOW.

WHEN we attend a lecture, we generally go to see the speaker not to hear what they have to say.

We know what they have to say. That's why we go to see them.

How many speeches have you heard? How many of them can you remember?

Words, words, words.

In a song, we remember firstly the melody and then we learn the words.

Instead of giving people the benefit of your wit and wisdom (words), try painting them a picture.

The more strikingly visual your presentation is, the more people will remember it.

And, more importantly, they will remember you.

A financial director.

A cash cow.

Even a financial director's speech doesn't have to be boring.

GETTING FIRED CAN BE A POSITIVE CAREER MOVE.

BEING fired often means that you are at odds with your company.

It means the job isn't right for you.

I have been fired five times, and each time my career took a step forward.

Being fired used to be a negative on your CV or résumé.

Now some headhunters find it an asset because it can show initiative.

A negative ...

... becomes a positive.

And now for a commercial break.

DOING A LAYOUT MEANS HAVING AN IDEA.

?

YOU have been commissioned to create a magazine ad for your client. All your efforts will be concentrated on finding a good idea.

The actual layout becomes a matter of fashion and taste. This is wrong.

Try treating the layout with the same intensity you bring to the main idea. Don't just arrange words and pictures. Invent a brand image for your client.

Invent a look that dramatizes the product or service you're selling without regard for fashion.

Place your magazine ad at the end of the corridor. It should be recognizable at a hundred paces, and it should be obvious who it's an ad for without seeing the brand name. However fleetingly a viewer may see the ad, they must have at least a subconscious realization that they've been exposed to that particular company's advertising. This is an invaluable benefit to your client.

In the example overleaf the brand name has been deleted. You should still know what it's advertising.

COMPOSE YOUR AD FROM THE WEAKEST POINT.

IF YOU know that your client's logo or product has to be big in an ad, don't hope that it will fit in the corner somewhere unobtrusively. It won't.

Start your layout knowing that it's a problem to be solved as an integral part of the idea.

Treat it as an advantage, not a problem.

There is a continuous battle between the client and the ad agency's creative department.

The client wants to advertise his name, his product and its benefits.

The creative person wants to advertise him or herself.

The creative idea is what the agency wants to explode on to the page.

The client would be happy with his logo.

Yet, oddly enough, they need one another.

The creative person has to have someone to sponsor his skill.

And the client knows that the creative mind increases sales.

Even Procter & Gamble recognize that.

The villain is not always the client. It is the fashion of the day that usually dictates the layout.

Be unfashionable.
Take risks.

Be like Stravinsky who said, *'I don't write music, I invent it.'*

ROUGH LAYOUTS SELL THE IDEA BETTER THAN POLISHED ONES.

1. IF YOU show a client a highly polished computer layout, he will probably reject it.

There is either too much to worry about or not enough to worry about. They are equally bad.

It is a fait accompli.

There is nothing for him to do. It's not his work, it's your work. He doesn't feel involved.

If he doesn't like the face of the girl in your rendering, or the style of the trousers worn by the man on the right, or your choice of the car he's driving, he will reject it.

He won't see the big idea. He will look at the girl's face and think, 'I don't like her, this doesn't feel right.'

It is very difficult for him to imagine anything else if what you show him has such detail.

2. Show the client a scribble.

Explain it to him, talk him through it, let him use his imagination.

Get him involved.

Because you haven't shown the exact way it's going to be, there's scope to interpret it and develop and change it as you progress.

Work with him rather than confronting him with your idea.

Uninvolved client.   Involved client.

IF YOU GET STUCK, DRAW WITH A DIFFERENT PEN.

CHANGE your tools, it may free your thinking.

For thirty years, I have been exposed to soulless layouts made with felt-tip pens on paper.

It's true, the plainness does help

focus on the idea, but it can also lead to dull layouts.

Instead, do your layouts in water-colours, charcoal, pencils, fountain pens with real ink. Use decorating paints and brushes. Blow up minuscule layouts, whatever you can think of.

It is not a solution, but it does open up the mind and it's fun.

I remember turning a £150,000 budget into a £200,000 budget just because I had done a watercolour storyboard.

It charmed the client and set a look for the whole project.

Different strokes for different folks.

SUPPLIERS ARE ONLY AS GOOD AS YOU ARE.

Don't hand your work over to a supplier hoping that they will produce the magic. They won't.

YOU are the magic.

The art of the art director is to get talented people to exceed their own capabilities.

It's difficult.

If you give a film director a free hand, he will do what he does because he thinks that's what you want from him.

It probably won't be.

You are employing him for the best thing on his reel or the one which is relevant to your job.

He may only have done one or two

great jobs in his life, and you're hoping to get a job of that standard.

Very unlikely.

If you brief him too tightly, it won't allow the freedom to make his work the thing you employed him for.

The art is to inspire him.

It's for you to have the vision that allows him to expand into something he hasn't done before.

It is the same with photographers, typographers, illustrators, directors, colour graders, editors, musicians and technicians.

It's for you to lead them along the path of enlightenment.

All will respond if you help show them a better way.

But you must show no fear.

It must be what you think, not what the client may think or your boss will think.

This is your job.

Don't refer back to those in authority, they will play for safety.

You're on your own. FLY OR DIE.

DON'T BE AFRAID TO WORK WITH THE BEST.

THE best people can be difficult. They are single-minded, they have tunnel vision. That's what makes them good. They are reluctant to compromise.

They can be intimidating, especially to the young, but if you approach them with an attitude that you want to do something well, they will respond positively.

Because they want to do something well too.

And if you are clear about what you want and strong about getting it, though there may be arguments, they will respect you (if not at the time, afterwards – I didn't say it was going to be easy).

The chances of you coming away with a superior job is not guaranteed, but it's greater than if you had worked with Mr Average Nice Guy.

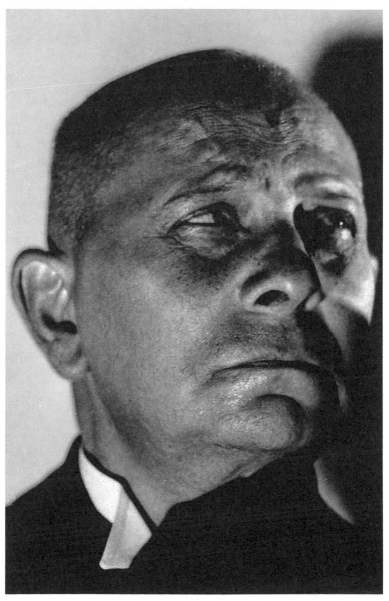

The film director Erich von Stroheim.
Loathed by many, loved by those who knew better.

GET OUT OF ADVERTISING.

ASK an advertising director who art directed a VW ad in 1989 and he'll tell you.

Ask him who the director of the National Theatre is and he won't know. Most advertising people live within the world of advertising.

90% of advertising inspiration comes from other advertising.

You will see the same books in every agency.

Certainly, a knowledge of the techniques and the tricks of advertising can be very useful, possibly essential.

True, people do look for something new, but sometimes it's something new to copy.

To be original, seek your inspiration from unexpected sources.

THE
ADVERTISING
ANNUAL

'THERE'S LESS HERE
THAN MEETS THE EYE.'
Tallulah Bankhead

DO NOT TRY TO WIN AWARDS.

NEARLY everybody likes to win awards.

Awards create glamour and glamour creates income.

But beware.

Awards are judged in committee by consensus of what is known.

In other words, what is in fashion.

But originality can't be fashionable, because it hasn't as yet had the approval of the committee.

Do not try to follow fashion.

Be true to your subject and you will be far more likely to create something that is timeless.

That's where the true art lies.

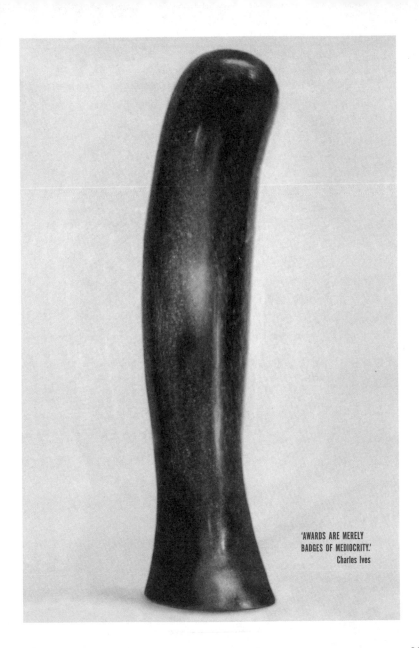

'AWARDS ARE MERELY
BADGES OF MEDIOCRITY.'
Charles Ives

*You don't have to be creative
to be creative.*

HOW YOU CAN MAKE YOUR COMPANY GREAT.

WE ALL want to be proud of the company we work for.

It enhances our reputation, makes us look good, feel good and gives us access to the best people.

The majority of us want to work for companies with glamorous reputations.

If you work for one of these companies, you are probably working for them for what they can do for you.

But not everybody is fortunate enough to be able to work for the outfit that is currently favoured.

So, given that not everyone in your company is an idiot, what are you personally going to do to make it company of the year?

Start by talking it up.

Begin thinking and behaving like a winner.

It will stop the rot. It will temporarily halt negative thinking and a defeatist attitude.

If you find people talking it down, take issue with them, tell others about them. If it persists, get them fired or, as a friend of mine did, fight somebody for talking disparagingly about the company he worked for.

People will soon get the idea.

Don't expect top management to lead the way. They are too busy running the company.

Decide you are going to make the company great; at least decide you are going to make a difference.

Observe that an organization's reputation is usually built on one or two key accounts.

Then pick the ground on which to make your assault.

Realize that companies' reputations are also built on one or two people. Aim to be that person or one of them.

You are halfway there. You have made the decision to do it. Now all you have is your wits, your talent, your guts and this little book to help you.

You are on your own. Just do it. Better.

HOW A SENIOR MANAGER CAN MAKE A BIG DIFFERENCE.

A BELGIAN agency I visited had a car account.

They had negotiated an agreement with the client.

95% of the budget would be spent servicing the client and giving him the advertising he thought he would want. The other 5% was spent by the agency doing the work the agency wanted, which the client was bound to accept.

What a good idea.

The client is happy because he gets given the work he wants with good grace.

The agency is happy because 5% of the creative freedom is far more exciting and rewarding than 100%

of a compromise, and they say what a great client.

By brokering an abnormal deal, the manager has made a huge difference to both creative standards and morale.

HOW A JUNIOR ACCOUNT HANDLER CAN MAKE A BIG DIFFERENCE.

IF YOU are working on a big corporate account, you can either hide behind the bureaucracy or you can use your initiative to further your agency's image and your own.

How? You may ask.

Ah, that's the fun, but here is an example.

You are in a position to manipulate money (I'm not talking large sums).

Set aside some money to be used for astonishing fresh creative work on a very small part of your account or accounts.

Speak to the very best creative people about doing some extra special work.

Get the creative director (if you trust him) to oversee the quality. Not to make it politically safe but to be creatively excellent.

With the money you have set aside, make the commercial.

Then show the client. He may not like it, but he may agree to pay for it to run somewhere.

If he doesn't, run it yourself. I believe there's a radio station in Ireland where peak time costs £60.

PR it. Enter awards if you have to.

If you fail, do it again.

Sure there's a risk. If you lose you get reprimanded, at worst fired.

But if you win ...

From being the lowliest of account people, you become the person creative people want to work with.

You are the person about whom the management say watch this space.

You become the new spirit of the agency.

HOW A MEDIA BUYER CAN MAKE A BIG DIFFERENCE.

MEDIA buyers have huge influence in where, when and in what form advertising is seen.

Their decisions are determined by statistics and logic and usually err towards the safe and dull.

For this reason, in my first job as creative director, I chose to share an office with the media director.

The advertising became more visible.

Putting a motorbike ad in a ladies' fashion magazine or even an ad for lingerie in a motorbike magazine may not be such a silly idea.

New business.

WHAT IS MEANT BY THE WORD 'CREATIVE'?

Put a value on this. *See back page for answer.*

THE word 'creative' is the currency with which ad agencies operate.

Without it there are no agencies.

It will feature heavily in any brief.

But what is meant by the word 'creative'?

It means something completely different to each client.

To one it may mean, 'I want the same as my competitors but different.'

To another it may be as simple as wanting a new jingle.

To another it means, 'Give me the same as we've had for the last twenty years, but not quite.'

99% will want something that they recognize from experience.

It has been alleged that Procter & Gamble's maxim is 'Creativity with a Precedent'.

Only one in ten thousand will really mean, 'Give me something I haven't seen before.'

So, before you make your pitch, find out exactly what your client means by the word 'creative'.

It's probably different from your definition.

HOW TO IMPROVE YOUR STRIKE RATE.

THE words 'creative pitch' signal party time for the whole creative department. It's an opportunity to relieve itself of the frustrating demands of ongoing clients.

It's an opportunity for everyone to show how clever they are. It is great fun, good for morale and hard for business.

A client will see up to five pitches, possibly on consecutive days.

That means he will see between five and ten campaigns, with twenty pieces of work in each campaign.

About 200 ideas in all, all of them competing for his attention.

To add to the confusion, every person on the client's side of the table has a different agenda as well as a difference of opinion about what is creative.

It's not surprising they make the

wrong decision.

So how can we help them make the right decision?

Lines (slogans) win business.

If you can find a way of summing up what the client wants to feel about his company but cannot express himself, you've got him.

He is yours.

Here are seven examples:

DRIVEN .... *Nissan*

THE WORLD'S FAVOURITE
AIRLINE .... *British Airways*

AUSTRALIANS WOULDN'T
GIVE A XXXX FOR ANYTHING
ELSE .... *Castlemaine XXXX*

IT IS – ARE YOU? .... *The Independent*

IT'S DIFFERENT OUT
HERE .... *Norwegian Cruise Lines*

WHY SLOW-MOW WHEN YOU CAN
FLYMO .... *Flymo Lawnmowers*

THE CAR IN FRONT IS
A TOYOTA .... *Toyota*

All these lines won the business because all of them made the chairman and staff proud to represent the company they worked for.

Repeat the line.
Repeat the line. Repeat the line.

Instead of covering the walls with different ideas, placing your slogan as an afterthought in the bottom right hand corner of the advertisement, make it an integral part of the headline.

Like this:

Or this:

It reduces the number of ideas presented from twenty to one.

Every advertisement you show is another opportunity to print your idea in the client's mind.

Wave the client's flag in front of him.

If, for instance, BP's logo is green and yellow, feature green and yellow in your presentation.

And if he's proud of his **LOGO** make it big. It may not please you aesthetically, but he'll find it reassuring to see his name.

Remember, advertising starts with a name.

Present creative work first.

How many times have you sat uncomfortably through media plans, research findings and planning strategies when all everyone wants to see is the creative work.

Try opening with the creative work. If he likes it he'll listen with interest to whatever else is said.

If he doesn't, you're dead anyway, and it will shorten the meeting.

Do not put your best people on new business pitches.

The most respected creative people will probably do something too original, too controversial to be acceptable to a conservative group of clients at your first meeting.

Put the people who consistently get the agency out of trouble on it.

Their work may not be as dazzling, but it will be intelligent and the client will relate to the idea better.

Finally. Present on Tuesday.

Assuming there are five pitches, on each day of the week.

By Friday the client will be so overwhelmed with the quantity and quality of work that he'll find it impossible to make a decision.

His thinking will go like this.

Monday – great meeting, great work, nice people.

Tuesday – great meeting, great people, nice work.

Wednesday – good meeting, very fresh work, lovely young people.

Thursday – yet another great meeting, nice people, fine work.

Friday – another meeting, I don't know.

The odds are that he will pick the Tuesday presentation, the second meeting because he was still clear-headed then.

Monday was too early, nothing to judge by.

Wednesday and Thursday were like eating too much chocolate.

Friday. Feeling sick.

Final thoughts.

MY FINEST HOUR.

I HAD been working with Richard Avedon in New York for a very ordinary client in the fashion industry.

The theme was African print dresses.

I wanted the models to be black and oily, dusty, dirty and wild. Leni Riefenstahl's Nuba woman was the brief.

Avedon asked me whether we could paint the models up, to which I said yes.

He then asked me if he could put the skirt on the head. I swallowed hard and said yes.

I didn't see the point of employing him and then not using him.

I suggested a wild pig in the background. He said no; the subject itself is the story.

A lesson in itself.

He seemed to be enjoying the

shoot, and I asked why he was so enthusiastic when he was in a position to do whatever he wanted to do all the time.

He said, 'It's not true Paul. I am employed by *Vogue* and they tell me what they want, and what they want is not always what I am interested in but I have a studio to run. So I do it.'

Quite an eye opener.

I was freer than he was.

After the shoot I walked out of the studio on 74th Street into a drizzly day with a yellow box of 10 x 8 Kodachromes under my arm.

I remember the moment vividly.

My feet seemed not to touch the pavement and I thought, 'I am going to be fired for these pictures.'

Would I rather be fired for having done them or not be fired having not done them?

There was no doubt in my mind. I would rather be fired.

Those few seconds on 74th Street

were my greatest moment in advertising.

When I got back and showed them to my partner he thought I was mad.

Fortunately the client loved them. 'This is art,' he said.

They won every award there was to be won.

The sad conclusion is the client got fired.

NOTES FROM THE PULPIT.

St Philip and All Saints Church, Birmingham.

I AM not qualified to speak about God. I am going to speak about advertising.

That is something I believe in.

When I mention that I am in advertising, people's instinctive reaction is that you are trying to sell people things they don't want.

They regard advertising as being a bit distasteful.

I am no more or less distasteful than you.

Yes, of course, I am selling. But so are all of you.

You are hustling and selling or trying to make people buy something. Your services or your point of view.

Tupperware parties, for example. They are selling.

You clean your car to sell it, showing it to its best advantage.

People even put bread in the oven to make their houses smell nice when they are trying to sell them.

The way you dress when going for an interview or a party, or merely putting lipstick on. Aren't you selling yourself?

Your priest is selling. He is selling what he believes in. God.

The point is we are all selling.

We are all in advertising.

It is part of life.

LIFE'S CREATIVE CIRCLE.

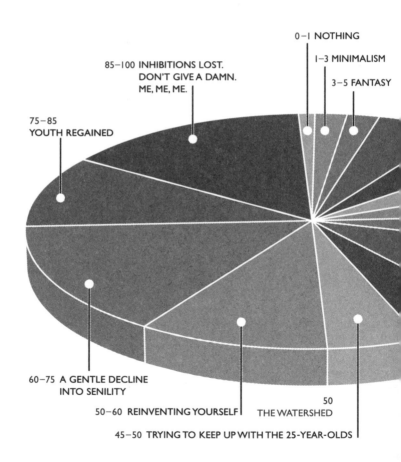

0–1 NOTHING

1–3 MINIMALISM

3–5 FANTASY

85–100 INHIBITIONS LOST.
DON'T GIVE A DAMN.
ME, ME, ME.

75–85
YOUTH REGAINED

60–75 A GENTLE DECLINE
INTO SENILITY

50–60 REINVENTING YOURSELF

50
THE WATERSHED

45–50 TRYING TO KEEP UP WITH THE 25-YEAR-OLDS

THE most popular conception of creativity is that it's something to do with the arts.

Nonsense.

Creativity is imagination, and imagination is for everyone.

Use this wheel to help you understand life's creative circle.

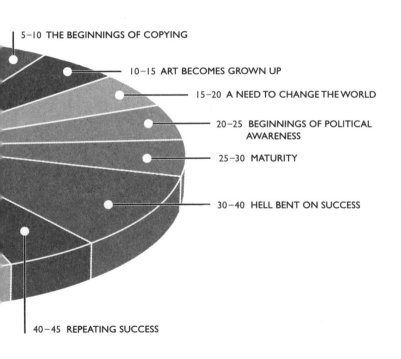

5–10 THE BEGINNINGS OF COPYING

10–15 ART BECOMES GROWN UP

15–20 A NEED TO CHANGE THE WORLD

20–25 BEGINNINGS OF POLITICAL AWARENESS

25–30 MATURITY

30–40 HELL BENT ON SUCCESS

40–45 REPEATING SUCCESS

WIT AND WISDOM.

'It's better to fail in originality, than succeed in imitation.' *HERMAN MELVILLE*

'Better nouveau than never.'
GROUCHO MARX

'Pink is the navy blue of India.'
DIANA VREELAND

'Success is going from failure to failure with no loss of enthusiasm.'
WINSTON CHURCHILL

'Early to bed. Early to rise. Work like hell and advertise.' *DR SCHOLL*

'The first thing to decide before you walk into any negotiation is what to do if the other fellow says no.' *ERNEST BEVIN*

'There are no short cuts to any place worth going.' *BEVERLY SILLS*

'Those who lack courage will always find a philosophy to justify it.' *ALBERT CAMUS*

'The superior man is distressed by his want (lack) of ability.' CONFUCIUS

'Some people take no mental exercise apart from jumping to conclusions.' HAROLD ACTON

'What the mind can conceive, the mind can achieve.' CLEMENT STONE

'Happiness is a singular incentive to mediocrity.' MICHEL MONTAIGNE

'Show me a sane man and I will cure him for you.' C G JUNG

'If everything seems under control you're not going fast enough.' MARIO ANDRETTI

'To become a champion, fight one more round.' JAMES CORBETT

'We don't see things as they are. We see them as we are.' ANAIS NIN

'Going to church doesn't make you a Christian anymore than going to a garage makes you a mechanic.' LAURENCE J PETER

Well, you've got to draw the line somewhere.

FOR A SHORT BOOK, A LONG LIST OF CREDITS.

ROGER KENNEDY, the designer of this book, has been the head of typography at Saatchi & Saatchi for twenty years.

I would find it difficult to fit his list of awards on this page.

He has been involved from the beginning of this book, not just with his typographical judgement but with his wit, both visually and verbally. For all his help I thank him warmly.

I wish to thank my old friend and mentor Christopher Macartney-Filgate, a contributor to this book and the first person to make me feel I wasn't quite as useless as I thought I was.

Thanks also to Jeremy Sinclair for letting me have the job that I wanted, his job, and then supporting me in it. Thanks also for his suggestion that I should add more pictures to this book.

To Andrew Cracknell for suggesting that I write this book.

To Michael Wharton for overseeing the writing and giving me helpful pointers.

To Cathy Heng for always coming to my rescue.

To Lucinda Roberts for her good nature and unflagging help throughout the process.

To Amanda Renshaw for believing in this book.

To Christian, Harriet, Sian and Ghokan, my loyal supporters.

To my friend and partner Nick Sutherland-Dodd, to whom I will be forever grateful.

Above all to my Father, my hero, who died in 2002 aged 98.

I should also like to extend my thanks to Alison Jackson, Graham Cornthwaite, Nancy Foutts, Richard Avedon, Melvyn Redford, Bob Carlos-Clark, John Pallant, Matt Ryan and Jade Trott for kindly letting me use their images.

Phaidon Press Limited
Regent's Wharf
All Saints Street
London N1 9PA

Phaidon Press Inc.
180 Varick Street
New York, NY 10014

www.phaidon.com

First published 2003
Reprinted 2003, 2004, 2005 (twice), 2006, 2007 (three
times), 2008 (twice), 2009, 2010, 2011
© 2003 Phaidon Press Limited

ISBN 978 0 7148 4337 7

A CIP catalogue record for this book is available from
the British Library.

Designed by Roger Kennedy
Printed in China

PICTURE CREDITS

Unless otherwise stated all images are courtesy Paul
Arden. Any inadvertent omissions can be rectified in
future editions. Original artwork by Lesley Arden/
Courtesy Paul Arden: 124–5; Photograph © Richard
Avedon: 114; Courtesy Graham Cornthwaite: 31;
Courtesy Doyle Dane Bernbach, New York: 37; Courtesy
Nancy Foutts: 118; The Kobal Collection/Paramount: 87;
The Kobal Collection/RKO: 47; Courtesy Mac McAloon:
15, 43; Courtesy Melvyn Redford: 29, 44; Courtesy
Schweppes/Photograph Alison Jackson/Camilla Shadbolt
as Victoria Beckham: 19; Courtesy Alex Thompson: 16;
Courtesy Jade Trott: 108; Courtesy Fraser Withers: 20–1.

Page 104: Value — nothing. It's rubbish, but something not too dissimilar was recently sold at
Sothebys for over £250,000.